The *Test* of a *Woman*

VOLUME 2

Letters to [MY] Father

Thoughts of a girl emerging into womanhood in the absence of her father.

SHAREYNA SCOTT JAMES

THE TEST OF A WOMAN: VOLUME 2

LETTERS TO [MY] FATHER

Shareyna Scott James

ISBN (Print Edition): 978-1-66783-168-8

ISBN (eBook Edition): 978-1-66783-169-5

Dedication

This book is dedicated to the little girl who lives inside all of us. May we continue to nurture and love her. To all of the fathers reading this, it is not too late. Your little girl needs YOU.

To My Father:

Howard John Scott, may you rest in peace. Thank you for the life lessons, showing me your love for people, and for beginning the legacy. I will take it from here. I pray I continue to make you proud.

–Rainy

*I am the daughter of black writers. We are
descended from freedom fighters who broke
their chains and they changed the world.*

–Amanda Gorman

Contents

Foreword

THERE COMES A TIME WHEN REFLECTION IS A NECESSARY PART of who we are. We stop and reminisce on the good and the bad, and if we are smart, we use those reflections to make us better. Stronger. As I sit and write, I am challenged to release some pivotal moments that have molded me into the woman I am today. If I am honest, not all of those moments felt good. Not all of those moments are easy to speak of. I can tell you the role a father plays (or not) in a young girl's life takes her far into adulthood, and those little inklings of him and the lessons are revealed over and over again. Those lessons become far more important as time goes on, and while the connections might not seem so clear, I challenge you to read this book with an open mind and heart. *Letters to [My] Father* is not just for women. It is, in fact, for fathers and soon to be fathers who strive to be better. While there is no manual for parenthood, I submit to you that resources such as these are what helps us to continue to be better, to know better, to love better. I encourage you to be reminded that it is okay to not get everything right all the time, but that constant working on self is necessary. It took some strength and courage to begin writing this book because of all that I knew it would entail. Addressing real-life conversations, ones that I have kept inside and have only allowed pieces out in conversation or in my dreams, and putting these words out into the atmosphere creates realness and allows for growth to take place. I challenge you to reflect on your own life's experiences and use this as an opportunity for your own reflection, growth, and forward thinking to what the life ahead could be. I invite you on this journey with me, and as you read, remember that the power in words not only lies within the author, but in the hands of the critics and readers who now have a glimpse into the mind of the author. I present to you *The Test of a Woman, Volume 2: Letters to [My] Father.*

A Note to My Older Self

I WISH YOU KNEW WHO YOU WOULD BECOME SO YOU WOULD worry less. I wish you understood the path God had you on and the impact you would make in the world. Stop stressing. It is going to be okay. You are going to be okay. Everything that was set in your path was for this moment right here. For you to accomplish this. This book is a larger part of your destiny, but you had to be frustrated to get here. You had to be disappointed to get here. There was no other way. In this very moment, you are free. You are unafraid, and you are releasing. Look at who you are right now. In the mirror. Get up, and look at you. Who would have ever thought you would speak so freely about these letters you had in you for so long? Certainly not you. But look. Here you are.

Smiling as you type, at peace with what was, and proud of who you are today. If no one tells you today, this week, or this month, I am proud of you. I got to see firsthand who we were becoming. And I watched you walk in fear, and doubt, and even shame, but I knew it was all for this purpose. I also watched you achieve some great things. I know you are still in awe when you think back, but I knew. I felt who you were becoming and I tried to get you to believe me. I knew it was a matter of time. You have learned to be so brave, when you were scared. You took risks, when your confidence was at an all-time low. You took what you had and you multiplied it. Do not ever forget who carried you. You alone could not have conquered such a feat. When people turned and left, the ones who just knew you would fall, when you felt alone but you knew you never were—yes those times. I saw you looking around, wondering, praying for life to be kinder. I'm proud to be your younger self. I wouldn't have traded it for anything in this world. Now, chin up, self-affirmations, we still have some work to do, but first, let's finish *The Test of a Woman: Volume 2!*

DEAR GOD,

Remind her that she is fearfully and wonderfully made. When she forgets how far she has come, remind her. Walk with her when she is afraid to take the next step. Keep her encouraged when fear surrounds her. Give her an extra sense so she knows when it's your will and not hers. Cover her life as she steps into this new realm. With every flaw, heal her. With every doubt, help her to embrace herself even more. Guide her, and when she refuses, push her—straight into greatness. Amen.

Author's Reflection

FATHERS, YOUR PRESENCE MATTERS. DESPITE WHAT SOCIETY may say or portray, the value that a father brings to a child is unmatched. While it may be popular for women to take on more in today's household, the role of the father has not changed. Our perspective of it may change, based on society's norms, but the fact of the matter is, households without fathers look very different. Now, let us not confuse a father's presence with someone who lives in a home but is not fulfilling his role. A father's role, if he chooses to operate in it, is powerful. He is the first example of how so many girls see what a man should look like in her life, how she should be treated (or not), but it forms her perspective, the conscious and the unconscious. While many would say why is the role of a mother not demonstrating the same? My response would be that young girls absolutely learn from their mothers, there is no argument there, but there are some facets of a young girl's life that operate in the realm of what she experiences and learns from the presence (or lack thereof) a man.

If you are a father reading this, I would encourage you to think about the men in your life. Set aside your thoughts or feelings of the men, but think about the qualities, abilities, and your innocent mind observing each man himself. Now, imagine this happening to a young girl who is born to her mother, but has this connection with a man who has a different level of speaking and understanding of life, from the male perspective. It is kind of hard to imagine this, but continue reading, and it will become more clear.

As little girls, we NEED our fathers. The very presence of them does something to us. We admire them. We look to them for guidance and strength. We want to know how we should be treated. But what if Daddy is not around. Absent? Does that mean we should feel less. . . loved? Should I not grow up to be a great woman if my Daddy does not tell me so?

The gift of a father, in some cases, is rare and sought after. So many women speak about the impact that fathers make, or men in general. I would encourage you to think about the women you know whose fathers had a great impact on their lives. What is your observation?

The Letters

My First LOVE

Approximate Age: 3 years old

Memory:

Riding my bicycle in front of our home. Cracked sidewalks. Small baby pool. Smiling, Happy, Me.

DEAR DADDY,

I am looking for you. I have this memory of riding my bicycle in front of the house, but I don't feel you near. I wonder if you have just gone to the store. No. You are not near. I can feel it. I wonder where you have gone. Do you not wonder where I am or how I am doing? I know you told me I was Daddy's little girl, but it does not seem like that today. My memory might be fading, but I would like to know if Daddy was near. Can you call me and ask for me?

Mommy is here. I can hear her calling for me from the window. She worries if I go too far. Daddy, do you not wonder? That just cannot be. I wish you were here with me, walking beside me so that I feel safe. But you are a memory.

When I go back inside, there are remnants of you. I can see your clothes. I see your cigarette butts in the ashtray, but I do not feel your presence. I do not hear your laughter. What about you and Mommy together. You are a part of our family, right Daddy?

I hope you are not upset that I am asking you all of these questions, but I want to know. Will you show up and protect me? I know you will. I just know it. It is time to go inside. It is getting dark. Dinner is almost ready. I can see Mommy has prepared it for us.

DEAR GOD,

Thank you for my family. Please keep Daddy safe. Amen.

Where Are You?

Approximate Age: 6 years old

Memory:

On stage. Just finished my very first on-stage performance in front of more than one hundred people.

DEAR DADDY,

I just finished my first recital! I did great! I was nervous, but I remember all that you said. Work hard, don't give up, be strong. I remembered all of the words and movements. Getting on stage, carrying those skates was a little scary at first. Mommy helped me up the steps, and she stood to the side of me so I wouldn't fall. I could feel her smiling at me. She made sure I could see her. I was one of the smallest on stage, but I made sure they saw me. I scooted to the front at the very end. You should have seen me! You would have been so proud.

Backstage was pretty crowded. Lots of clothes scattered on the floor, hair bows, beads, shoes, and of course my roller skates were all tangled. I can hear Mommy calling me, "come on grab your stuff, it's time to go!"

In the backseat of the car, I sat quietly, wondering if Mommy would say something else. Not about my performance but about where you are. It feels like just yesterday we were having breakfast, and I listened to you and Mommy talking. But that seems far away. I decide to ask, "Mommy, is Daddy home?"

"No, he's not home."

I hoped she would say more. I hope you are on your way home. Maybe you are working late. Yes, that's it. You are working. Well, see you soon, Daddy.

DEAR GOD,

I wish my daddy was there to see me today. He says to pray whenever I have questions about things I don't understand. Is my daddy with you, God? If he is, keep him safe and tell him I'll be up at 7:00 a.m. to see him, and I hope he's home by then. Amen.

I've Got This!

Approximate Age: 7 years old

Memory:

Sitting in the kitchen, counting pieces of candy, 1, 2, 3, . . . 10, place candy in a bag, repeating until I get to ten bags.

Dear Daddy,

Okay Daddy, I've got this! I did exactly what you told me to do. I sorted the candy by flavors, and counted them one to ten and then bagged them. I'm ready to go and see if I can sell them and earn some money to go to the store. I would rather be playing with my Barbie dolls or outside exploring, but you said this is what I have to do. You and Mommy always tell me not to talk to strangers, but I guess now it's okay. I gather up all the bags I put together, and I'm ready to go! I ask my sisters to come with me, but they all say no.

Now I'm angry that I have this assignment in the first place. Why don't they have to go? I just want to go and play with my toys.

Daddy, I thought you would come with me. I thought you would teach me all I need to know about being my own businesswoman. Nope. Wrong again. I'm not sure I understand why I have to figure this all out on my own. But I guess I have no choice.

I do as you tell me, and I go door to door. You told me to sell the candy for $1, but every time someone opens the door, the person either does not want the candy and just gives me $1 or the person does want the candy but instead of $1, he or she gives me $5. I sit down at the kitchen table when I get home and I count my money—$100! Wow, that's a lot of money! I've never seen that much money before.

So, it's that easy to make money. You come up with an idea and boom—$100? Thanks, Daddy. I'll be sure to remember this the next time I have a bright idea.

DEAR GOD,

Thank you for letting my dad teach me about making money. I know this doesn't all make sense to me now, but he's trying, I can see that. So, can you keep him around to teach me some more things like this? I had fun AND I made a lot of money for a kid my age. Okay, off to the store I go! Thanks, God. Amen.

Life Lesson

Approximate Age: 8 years old

Memory:

Sitting at my desk at a brand-new school. Looking around to see not one person looking like me.

DEAR DADDY,

I don't really understand why we had to move—again. It feels like every time I start to make new friends, I have to say goodbye. Daddy, I am really tired of saying goodbye all the time. I wish I understood why we can't just be in one place for more than a year. I might as well just never unpack and live out of boxes. I thought life was supposed to go a little more like this:

1. You are born into an amazing family who love and care for you. (I have questions about where our family is, but I'll get to that later.)

2. You have the cutest little nursery where you are adored and eventually grow from your crib to your toddler bed. (I'll have to ask Mommy if this ever existed because I do not remember any remnants of this.)

3. You attend school, make lots of friends, and have the best birthday parties one could remember. (My parties are the BEST, but I have questions about the friends I'm supposed to have.)

4. You get older, and you finally get that teenage bedroom you've had your eye on every time you visit the furniture store.

Daddy, how will I EVER get to #4 if we keep moving. I turn and notice a girl who had some similar features to mine, light eyes, brown-ish skin, semi-curly hair. I say hello to her, and she looks as if she was looking right past me. Everyone else around me was white. I was, for the first time, an outcast. I didn't really understand why I was the outcast, but this very moment replayed itself in my life several times over. This moment was needed and I didn't even know it.

Daddy, I guess you are trying your best to give us a better life by moving here. It doesn't make sense to me. Don't you think you could have at least moved where there were more people who look like me? They have so many questions about my hairstyles and skin tone that I can't answer. Maybe, just maybe, you'll feel the same and we can move—again. But where to now

Daddy? Where to …

DEAR GOD,

I know my dad loves me, he tells me all the time. But sometimes I really don't understand why he makes decisions and then changes his mind in just a short time. Why doesn't he ask me how I feel or what I think? I really wish he would. Is my opinion not valuable? Amen.

Scared

Approximate Age: 9 years old

Memory:

Lying under a blanket at my mom's best friend's house. Mommy has a bat, my sister is angry, I'm not sure where Daddy is, but I'm sure he's near.

DEAR DADDY,

I don't look at the calendar everyday, but it feels like it's been awhile since I've seen you. Mommy doesn't really say much, and no one will tell me anything because "I need to stay in a child's place." But we rushed to Mommy's friend's house, and now I'm sleeping on the couch. I feel safe with Mommy near, but you are not. I don't really understand why you always seem so far away. When you are home it's just different. But you don't ever stay long. I wish you would help Mommy feel okay. She seems scared. I know this means we are probably moving again because whenever we go somewhere so quickly, we always end up moving soon after.

I hope you can help me make some sense of this because none of my friends seem to be moving like this. Oh, and where is our family? I haven't seen them much either. Mommy's friend came and made us breakfast and handed me the remote control to watch some television. I thought to myself, "this isn't so bad, I guess. I don't have to clean my room or do any chores right now, so I guess staying here is pretty cool."

A few weeks go by, and Mommy shows us our new place to live. I have my own room, with fluffy carpet, and there's a whole lot of kids in this neighborhood. And get this, they all look like me! Mommy said I can decorate my room however I want. I'm happy to be here, Daddy, there is so much space and a park right outside! But Mommy says you aren't coming to live with us.

Something isn't right, but I can't ask questions, so I hope you find my diary, magically. Where are you now, and what is happening to our family? Does this mean there will be no more big family parties where all of the cousins get to play into the night? What will happen to you teaching me about being my own boss? Who will teach me all of those things? And what about your drums? Whose lap will I sit on and listen to them play? Well, those are the questions I have for now. I hope you're coming soon ...

DEAR GOD,

I never knew I could be happy and sad all at once. I love my new room. Mommy painted it herself. It feels weird without Daddy though. God, I hope I make some new friends here and that we don't move again for a very long time! Can you talk to Mommy to make sure of it? I hope you can hear me! Amen.

New School

Approximate Age: 10 years old

Memory:

Multicultural day at school. Bring in a dish that represents your heritage.

DEAR DADDY,

Today in class, my teacher asked us to come prepared to share a piece of our heritage with the class. I have to admit, I was stumped. Here's how it went:

> Okay, class, on Friday, I would like everyone to bring in a dish that represents your culture and where you come from. It can be a meal, a dessert, anything you would like. I can't wait to see all of the representation in our class!

I gulped a giant gulp in my throat. I was unsure of exactly what my teacher was asking. I really didn't have an understanding of where my people came from, let alone the cultural foods they ate. I thought about my mom's upbringing in New Orleans, but I didn't have much understanding about my dad, except that he was from a town called New Rochelle in New York. What type of food represents New York?

I went home that day feeling frustrated, after listening to my classmates talk about their Irish, German, Italian, and Haitian backgrounds. I couldn't ask my dad because, well, I hadn't seen him in months. He normally would have lots of stories for me whenever I would ask him a question.

He was like a walking book. Mommy was always so busy trying to care for us, cooking, cleaning, preparing for the next day, and taking care of the baby cat I surprised her with one day (I still think she wasn't too happy about that decision that me and my dad made, without her permission). So, I sat stumped in my room until my mom came knocking and asked me what was wrong.

"Mom, I don't know about my heritage, where do our people come from? Our teacher asked us to bring in a cultural dish and I don't even know what to bring in. My favorite food is lasagna, but that's Italian. I love fried chicken, but is frying chicken really heritage?"

"Well, we do have foods that we eat that are created from our people. Our heritage is complicated, and some day I'll explain it to you better so you can understand. Let me tell you about a dish that's made in New Orleans called gumbo. I make it every year at Thanksgiving and there's a history behind it."

> *Our people used whatever food was leftover to make a soup that would last for days and could feed an entire family. Veggies, seafood, chicken, meat, you name it, it's in gumbo. You can bring in this dish with a little rice and explain that our people have a rich history, particularly from New Orleans, Louisiana, and this dish is a reminder of that heritage and is served throughout the city.*

"How does that sound?"

"Wow, Mom, I never knew there was a history behind that meal. I always wondered why there were so many ingredients in it. I can't wait to share this with my class!"

Dear God,

I pray that one day I understand why my people were treated so badly. I just don't understand why it had to be us or anybody for that matter. Amen.

Failure

Approximate Age: 11 years old

Memory:

Receiving my sixth-grade report card/progress report.

Dear Daddy,

I was doing so well in school. I was actually one of the few kids who loved school and having homework. Reading is my absolute favorite subject—I love being able to explore with characters and imagining what it would be like to be in their world. I think I'll be a writer some day! I always have so many questions. You always say "I talk too much," and you call me motormouth more times than I can count.

Mommy can't seem to figure out why my report card is filled with Cs and Ds and an F. An F! How is the little girl who loves to ask questions coming home with an F on her report card? I didn't have an answer for Mommy, but suddenly, when she asked me "what was wrong with what she saw," I felt the urge to say, "I miss Daddy." I know that wasn't the answer to her question, but it was the first thing that came to mind. And it's true, I do miss you Daddy.

I was scared when I had to sit down with my teachers and Mommy about my report card. I knew that I wasn't doing my best. I was disappointed in myself but I really didn't want to go to school. Nothing seemed right without you around. And . . . When I looked around, there was no shortage of dads. I couldn't understand why you were not there.

And then . . . in you walked into the guidance counselor's office. Disappointed and upset with me. How could this be? All I wanted was to see you, but not like this. Not with you mad at me. I have never seen you so upset with me about my grades.

"Now, you know better than to bring home these kinds of grades. I expect more from you. You are too smart and this is unacceptable. I expect nothing but greatness from you moving forward. You got it? I mean it. Don't have me come back up to this school little girl."

"Yes Daddy, I promise. I'll do better—you watch. I'm going to make you so proud." I guess I didn't even think you cared since you're never around to help with homework or projects. I wish I could say all of this to you, but I'm too afraid you'll disappear again so I'll keep my thoughts to myself. But I'm listening to everything you say. I will do better, for you and for Mommy, although I know Mommy won't leave if I do bad in school, you just might. So, now I have to work extra hard so you are proud and hopefully you won't disappear again.

DEAR GOD,

You have some explaining to do. I don't understand where Daddy was and how he showed up all of a sudden. I'm too afraid to ask him, but I sure am happy he's back. I know he won't ever live with us again (Mommy said so), but I hope he doesn't just come around when my report card is bad. Anyway, I know I can do better, and I will. Oh and God, can you keep Daddy around? I feel much better when I know he's there. Amen.

Patience

Approximate Age: 13 years old

Memory:

Sitting on the right arm of the couch, waiting
for Daddy to pick me up for the weekend.

DEAR DADDY,

The weekend is here, and that means that I am going to your house. I will be able to play pretend with all of your office supplies, help you answer phone calls, and of course at the end of the night, I can sit and listen to you play the drums like old times. It's 8:58 p.m. and I can see Mommy pacing back and forth. She seems a little annoyed. I have my backpack on, coat on, because you said you would be here by 8:00 p.m.

You're usually always late, so I told Mommy not to worry and to just go to bed. I heard her on the phone, faintly in the kitchen, but I couldn't hear what she was saying. The television show I was watching ended and now the ten o'clock news is on. I think I must have dozed off. I look around at the time and realize I'm still sitting on the couch. No sign of Daddy. I hear footsteps, and it's Mommy, insisting that I go to bed this time. I ask her if I can call you one last time.

Ring . . . ring . . . ring . . . Hello, you have reached my voicemail. Please leave a message after the tone. This can't be. Mommy was right—again. Why would Daddy not show up? Why would he not call? I didn't want to go upstairs because that meant that he really wasn't coming. I open the door to look outside just one more time. I come back inside, and Mommy offers me a hug and says, "I'm sorry." I really didn't understand why she would be sorry. She didn't do anything. She made it seem as though it was her fault that Daddy didn't show up. I hug her back and walk upstairs to my room. I lie in my bed, and tears begin to roll down my face. I'm sad. I can't even say that I'm angry because the emotion is definitely sadness. I see so many daddies show up for their daughters, but why not mine? Why does my daddy not show up, not call, and just leaves me sitting and waiting on the couch for hours? I'm just really sad that my life looks different from my friends, and I just want it to be normal! Why can't my life be normal?

At 8:00 a.m. the next morning, my mom walks into my room and says, "your father is outside." I grab my bag and walk to his car, which reeks of cigarette smoke and some other smell. The coffee cup from Dunkin' Donuts and 20 oz. Coca Cola sit in the cup holder, and Daddy looks like he hasn't been asleep all night. His eyes were so red. We get to the first stoplight, and Daddy doesn't move when the light turns green.

"Daddy, Daddy, are you asleep? Wake up, the light is green!" Daddy speeds up, and I look at him to be sure he's awake. It's snowing outside, and I can see the snow falling off of the trees, onto the car. BOOM! "Daddy!!" A giant mass of snow hits the windshield and wakes Daddy up again. He gets out of the car to clean it off and asks if I mind if he keeps the window down so he can have some fresh air to keep him awake. "Yes, Daddy, whatever you need to stay awake. We have a long drive."

DEAR GOD,

I have a question. Why did you choose my daddy for me? He doesn't do what other daddies do. He doesn't show up when he's supposed to and makes promises he doesn't keep. Why do I have a daddy who doesn't show up? Why couldn't I have a daddy like all of my other friends? Maybe one who actually lived with me? Maybe one who kept his promises? Oh, and my daddy really needs to get some sleep. I was a little scared this time when he fell asleep behind the wheel. Amen.

I Believe You

Approximate Age: 20s

Memory:

A decade of reflection

To My Father,

As a woman now, there are so many questions I have about life that I now know I may never get the answer to. I know that many of the decisions I have made were from me being naive, not listening when you or Mommy said no, and some were from being just plain old stupid. Now, I know that I could have come to talk to you, but sometimes you honestly just weren't around or you didn't have the time. I have to admit that I was frustrated when I would see people around me whose fathers were front and center in their lives. And I was angry with you for a long time. I always heard that there was a sickness you had, but you seemed fine to me. Every time I saw you, you were just fine. Your business was thriving. You made sure I knew that you were a self-made millionaire. I've seen you open several businesses. I've seen the awards, the accolades. You were great at what you did. There was no denying that. I was proud of your accomplishments. But I questioned your love for me. When I sat back and looked at the moments when you weren't around, I honestly couldn't understand. If someone loved you, how and why would he miss those special moments? Why did you have me in the first place? All of this reflection made me angry all over again. I just didn't understand and no one wanted to explain it to me. I was Daddy's little girl, which also didn't make sense because it was the four of us, until the fifth one came. How could I be Daddy's little girl when you never showed up for me?

I wish you would have sat me down and explained "the birds and the bees" or at least one bird. Something. I thought that just maybe if I had the answers to my questions, then my twenties might have looked different. I distinctly remember writing down what I wanted my life to look like. I sat at the kitchen table and I did it. I had a vision, and some things on there I made up. I guess I needed a playbook showing me how to make some of that happen. I remember you coming to my first apartment and sitting me down for hours to give me some advice. You must have thought that I was making a lot of mistakes because you've never sat me down for that long. I vaguely remembered bits and pieces, but I remember us crying together and me getting some strength back. I was still angry with you, but I didn't tell you. I was too afraid you would leave or worse. So, I kept it in, but I said one day, I'm going to write it all down and tell you.

In my twenties, I didn't really understand your sickness. I thought it was an excuse for you not wanting to be a father. I thought that anyone could stop something if they wanted to. I was naive. I think you were either too ashamed to talk about it or maybe the pain of talking about it made you want to go back to your vice. So, I never brought it up. I only thought about it. You struggled to get to my events and my kids' birthday parties, and for that I'm grateful. I had to do some work to manage our relationship and protect myself so I wouldn't get hurt over and over like when I was a child. I wanted to understand now, though. Watching your life was heartbreaking. I knew what you had in you. I had seen you bounce back so many times. While I didn't really understand what it took for you to bounce back, I was proud of you, and I told you so. After not having the answers and wanting you to be free, we had a silent understanding that I would only ask but so much and you would only give but so much, but you wanted me to know that you loved me. And finally, I believed you.

DEAR GOD,

It took me up until this point in my life to somewhat understand what my father was going through. I am grateful that he is still here for me to talk to, but I have to be honest that every time someone calls or texts me about him I'm concerned. I'm hoping it's not "the call." I'm finally able to express my hurt, frustration, and anger out loud, as I know I want to forgive him before it's too late, but I can't help but feel like if he had just been there, then maybe I might not have had to go through all that I have. I'm going to need some help at rebuilding this relationship with my father, one with no expectations. If I don't have any expectations I can no longer be hurt, right? God, help him, heal him, and make him whole. Amen.

Understood

Approximate Age: early 30s

Memory:

Life as I know it. Today. Right now.

DADDY,

I understand. Up until this point in my life, I have had a lot of emotions and thoughts about my childhood and the why behind my life. Looking from the outside, many people would say that my life wasn't so bad. And honestly, it wasn't so bad. But, from the perspective of a child, it looked very different from those around me. I had always hoped that you and Mommy would get back together. When I looked around as a young girl, there were some things missing that I didn't quite understand. I missed having family dinners, holiday activities, and visiting with aunties, uncles, and cousins on random Saturdays. I was always looking for what wasn't there. Honestly, I was frustrated as a little girl. As I continued to grow, I always asked questions. I wanted to know everything about everything. I believe this is what has helped me to develop such a love for education. While things might have been frustrating in one aspect of my life, I continued to put my energy into my love for more. Wanting more, doing more, asking more, giving more, learning more. I know that I got much of my entrepreneurial interests from you.

I see so much of my life's work in who you were. It's funny how the things I didn't so much care for as a child, I not only have implemented myself but also I have ingrained much of them into my own career and personal life. I finally can say that I understand. I may not know every detail or every why, but I know enough to know that nothing you did was intentionally to hurt me. I didn't believe that previously. I thought that a father could not possibly love his daughter who he didn't call regularly, didn't see regularly, and didn't show up for—on time, regularly. I couldn't see how I watched Mommy struggle for years and it wasn't intentional on your part. I knew your heart, but it never made sense to me. I understand now. As a child you couldn't talk to me, and as an adult, I'm sure you were ashamed of having not been there and realizing it was too late.

The physical conversation never happened, but I kept the questions, the memories for this point in time. I knew that one day I would let it all out. Though, I didn't want to be angry when I did. I love you Daddy, forever and always. I just pray that you have been able to forgive yourself and make peace with what didn't.

I've had to make peace with my childhood. Complaining about what was missed only does one thing—rob me of today. It doesn't bring it back nor does it change anything. I still think about it from time to time, but now, I make the choice to change the things that I can.

DEAR GOD,

When I was young, my dad always shared the Serenity Prayer with me.

> *God, grant me the serenity to accept the things I cannot change.*

> *The courage to change the things I can.*

> *The wisdom to know the difference.*

I can remember being seven years old reciting this prayer, and I thought it was the silliest thing because I had no idea what I was saying. When I was twenty-seven, I decided to get my first tattoo and it has the word *Serenity*. I still don't think I quite knew how much that word would resonate with me. But now, as I sit and read the prayer quietly to myself, I get more meaning every time. There were so many things I harbored about my childhood, things I didn't understand and I mostly blamed on Daddy. There were things I'm sure he would have changed if he could, starting with himself. He had some courage and definitely some wisdom. He needed some help with the tools and how to put it all together. God I know that you were and are the only tool that can do this for any of us. Grant me wisdom, courage, serenity, and most of all continued understanding as I go through life with the memory of my father. Amen.

A Note to My Younger Self

Baby girl. I need you to look at me. Don't get up. Sit right there and look. You have more than you need, and you don't even know it. You are a product of some strong people, and I'm not talking about your ancestor's blood. Your parents. You keep asking God why you seem so different from everyone around you. Why does your life look so different? You're right, it does look different, but I don't know that it looks so different. There are some things you are not meant to understand just yet. What you will learn is that all of this will make sense later in life. I know you are upset baby girl, and that's okay. You are allowed to be. What I want you to know is that when you feel alone, because you will, when you feel afraid, because you will, when you are upset, because you will be, talk to God. The most important relationship you will have in this life is with God. So, tell him everything. You can cry to him, yell, all of it, and he's got your back.

Stay focused. You have set yourself apart without even knowing it. That drive that you have to do well is something that you will never lose. It's in you. Trust me, you are going to need it in a few years and for the rest of your life. Get those grades and push yourself, always. This too is going to pay off. Oh, and stop worrying so much. What I can tell you is that worrying is not going to help you, nor will it fix anything. I know it's easier said than done, but you have to stop.

Stop doubting yourself. Stop looking around at other people, wishing and wondering. Your path was uniquely made for you. You have everything that you need, and then some. Trust me, just trust me. What you don't have, you don't need. The rest of what you need will be provided to you. You will vaguely remember my words, but as long as you hold on to them, that's what's most important. Self-doubt will always try to creep in and remind you of your failures or what you lack. It will try to bring you backward. The thing about self-doubt is that it will always try to creep in when you are having a rough day or are troubled. It will try to remind you that you can't do something or you don't have what it takes. You can know all of this but still doubt yourself, and you will. If you remember nothing else, remember that your life is perfect just the way that it is. It is up to you to use all of what you have to your greatest ability. Try not to be so hard on yourself. Life will be hard enough.

Wisdom. You will hear this word throughout your life, and it is probably one of the words that you will not understand until much later. It sounds great on the surface, but the reality is, wisdom is hard to access. It requires a level of growth and understanding and a commitment to yourself to want to be better. To do so, you have to be willing to listen to what others say and don't say. You have to be willing to do some things that might make you comfortable just so that you can grow. While you may come into contact with some people, and you may not particularly agree with their life choices or who they portray themselves to be, they too will have some wisdom for you. Wisdom isn't always this exciting, powerful thing. What you do with it is what will make you wise. How you choose to maneuver through life using your experiences and those of others is what wisdom is all about. Don't believe me? You will, soon. Remember this, the way you will know it's wisdom is that you will recall an instance in your life that will be a reminder or a glimpse of something you overlooked where there was a lesson or something that you could have held on to. Little pieces of wisdom are just as important as those little lessons. A word to the wise . . .

Make yourself a promise.

1. Promise to not be so hard on yourself.

2. Promise to allow yourself to hurt.

3. Promise to allow yourself to heal.

4. Promise to allow yourself to love.

5. Promise to allow yourself to forgive.

Baby girl, hold these five promises close. You will need them for the rest of your life.

Love,

Your Older Self

DEAR GOD,

Help her to know that she is "fearfully and wonderfully made." Help her to hold on to you when there is nothing else to hold on to. Help her to look up, instead of looking down. Help her, heal her, give her wisdom, guide her, and never let her go, Amen.

The Reflections

Forgiveness

FORGIVENESS. SOME WOULD ARGUE, THIS IS ONE OF THE MOST difficult words in the English language. Many express it in its most simplistic form, and in theory it sounds so easy to do. Essentially, you experience hurt, said individual who hurt you says sorry, you say okay, and forgiveness has been achieved. There is just one problem with this scenario. It does not work this way. In fact, forgiveness is not accomplished by words only. It is actually an action, many times ongoing, that requires an individual to consciously choose to focus on the present and future. If, at any moment, the individual decides to live back in the past where hurt was, there is a possibility what was once forgiven can be undone. This is a powerful exchange that can truly have lasting effects on relationships, generations even. The thing about forgiveness is that usually, the act that caused forgiveness to be necessary in the first place cannot be undone. Herein lies the dilemma.

Being stuck in a past state, whether one wants to admit it or not, usually has some impact on the individual's ability to move on 100 percent. If there is always something in the way, consciously or unconsciously, there is a turmoil that exists within the individual. We could go on and on about forgiveness, but that is not the reason why I am writing this to you. For many of us, true forgiveness, in action, not in words, can take years. Peeling back the layers of the wrongdoing, and then the emotion tied to it, can be a roller coaster in itself. The power of forgiving others really is a choice you have to decide to make for yourself.

As I write this, I remember years and years of anger that came before me forgiving my father. I was angry at what could have been and the life that I imagined but never became my reality.

I tell you this, when I stood up to speak at my father's funeral, I was grateful that I had forgiven him—for all of the parts of him that I did not understand and for the critical moments in my life where I missed his presence. I was grateful that I forgave him because what I can say in this moment is that while forgiving may hurt, not forgiving when it is too late is a much worse pain. It was hard to forgive when there was never a sorry or a make up, but it is possible. The thing is, now, after having so many unanswered questions and having asked God to help me accept what I have, made me realize that while I had some hurt, a lot of hurt actually, so did my father. I never wanted to hurt him, so I held on to so many questions.

{Step} Fathers

THE ONLY FATHER SOME GIRLS WILL EVER HAVE MAY HAVE THE title of Stepfather. The name itself implies there is something added here. The role of a stepfather may vary from house to house, but there are some little girls (and grown women) who would say that the role that their stepfather played in their life was pivotal to their growth and support. They matter. Stepfathers might feel rejected when they first meet the daughter(s) of their mate. Sometimes, this rejection is filled with anger that the daughter herself might not understand. This anger could come from not having her own father, having an abusive father, wanting her mother to herself, and the list could go on. The role of a stepfather in the home is unique, I would imagine, as the man's role as a husband naturally requires him to lead and provide, but often-times, stepfathers are stripped of this. Being expected to do a role that is often scrutinized within and outside of the home is undoubtedly challenging.

More often now we see this role becoming the norm in many households. If you ask some stepfathers, they will tell you that the role is rewarding. If you ask others, they will say they will gladly give the role back to the men who they borrowed it from. There are countless instances where the stepfather has replaced the father altogether in the home. Some women say that having a stepfather was such a blessing to them, while others say it ruined their lives.

Now, this is one perspective you are about to read. However, before I say my next thought, I want to first say that if there is an unhealthy relationship with your stepfather, you can feel free to disregard what I am about to say next and skip to the next piece of this book as this is section is not meant to validate any inappropriate behaviors or relationships that might exist as we know they do.

Stepfathers MATTER. If allowed and if desired, this role can be pivotal in the life of a young girl (and woman for that matter). In the absence of a father, a stepfather has the unique ability to provide that safety and support where it might not exist. This does not take away from the role that mothers play in the home, but where there is a void, it can be filled. If there is no void, and there is a healthy relationship with the birth father, this can provide another opportunity for there to be added love in a child's life. Some might argue that the whole construct of a man in the home who is not the girl's father is a recipe for chaos, but there are some people reading this right now saying, "I thank God for my stepfather!" And, there are some stepfathers saying, "I thank god for my stepdaughter!" You see, any role that someone plays in life can be looked at as good or bad. The reality is that some stepfathers have been the only fathers some girls ever knew. Some of them have stepped up in ways that they did not have to, but because of love they did.

If you are a stepfather reading this book—thank you. The title itself does not sound glorifying, and you might feel like you are undervalued. And while this is no consolation for how you might be feeling, I want to say thank you. You have the opportunity to add value and in many instances to change a young girl's life for the better. That is not to say it will be without trials, but the role of a birth father is not either. Love the stepdaughter that you have. She might need a father in her life more than she knows. Be encouraged. I cannot make any promises, but I can almost guarantee there is a girl (or woman) reading this right now shaking her head and saying, "I wouldn't be where I am today without my stepfather!" Now, if your relationship with your stepdaughter is not so great, it is not too late to try. If there is even a glimpse of hope, then there is a possibility that change can take place. Society has labeled the role of a stepparent not always in the best light, unfortunately. The name itself implies that there is a backstory to what happened with the relationship with the birth parents. At this moment, right now, forget about all of what happened between adults. If you want to have a better relationship with your stepdaughter, try. While I know I have only spoken about the positive side of this role, I know there are some situations where stepfathers regret their decision. If love were only enough. I wish I could say more than "I'm sorry that was your experience," but as with all roles in life, there are no guarantees.

Addiction

IT IS AMAZING HOW MUCH THE IMPACT OF ONE WORD CAN HAVE on a person's life. A word that brings about a variety of emotions at any given moment. A word that brings about memories that are often painful and harmful. A word that has broken up families, separated generations of people. One word has so much power, or is it that we give it power? A word that is only understood over time for many. *Addiction* (n) is defined as a compulsive, chronic, physiological or psychological need for a habit-forming substance, behavior, or activity having harmful physical, psychological, or social effects and typically causing well-defined symptoms (such as anxiety, irritability, tremors, or nausea) upon withdrawal or abstinence (Merriam-Webster Collegiate Dictionary, 2003). If I scroll down and look at additional meanings of what an addict is, I find that there are several, including a person who has become physically or psychologically dependent on a chemical substance. This is in no way a research project on addiction, nor is it meant to serve as a resource for addiction defined, but rather this is an examination of the impact that addiction has on the lives of those who are bound by it.

I recall going to meetings with my father and having a smorgasbord of snacks to choose from for an entire hour. I never listened to what they were saying, except the introductions where everyone went around the room and said, "Hi my name is ___, and I am an addict." I never thought twice about where I was, nor did I care, because I did whatever I wanted for the sixty minutes. Now, there are a few things that I can say (now that I am adult):

1. Why was I attending the meetings in the first place without a filter on what I might hear?

2. My dad was fully aware of his addiction and was trying to seek help and community.

3. Why was there not a group for kids who attended to better understand addiction?

4. Did my mom know I was at these meetings?

What I do know is that, having had a parent who is an addict, having a better understanding of what addiction can mean for the family unit is critical. While I did not understand his struggles, having some context of sickness might have helped me not be so angry all the time! It might have helped me to understand that some of his behavior was out of his control. As an adult, it all makes sense why he missed so much of my life, the smells from his car, the sleepless nights, the outbursts, and why Mommy left. These conversations are hard to have not only with yourself, but I cannot imagine having to have them with your child. The shame and disappointment every time the addiction takes over. Because my dad had an addiction did not mean that he did not love me. It meant that he was not in control of himself or his behaviors. While there are many who would argue that he could have and should have figured out a way (and I will admit that I was one of those people), the reality is those are opinions, and he did not shake his addiction.

The reality is that I grew up with a father who had some internal struggles that impacted everyone around him. And my story is not the only one of its kind. In fact, there are far too many stories like mine. The purpose of talking about addiction here is to share the real truth behind much of this book. All of the letters were written with an "elephant in the room." Where was Daddy? Why was he not present. Too often, we do not want to use the word addiction. When I found out my dad was an addict, I never would say the word out loud, I would just say, "he's sick or he has a problem." I never wanted to openly admit that my dad was "different." What I came to learn was that not only did my dad suffer from drug abuse but he also suffered from alcoholism. The level of addiction only worsened over time.

I will end this section with this. No one, unless an addict themself, will ever truly understand what it takes for someone struggling internally with addiction to have to live with it every single day, on top of life's other cares and worries. Be gentle, as best you can, be kind as much as you can, and look to forgive even when an apology may never exist. And finally, if you are reading this and do not suffer from addiction, be thankful that you have had the strength to live without.

Healing

WITH ALL THAT LIFE THROWS AT US AND WITH ALL OF THE HELP that we might receive from others, the one thing that no one can do for us is heal. We have to take steps, which include forgiveness and letting go, in order for healing to take place. Healing is a gradual process that cannot happen overnight. Just like with a wound, it takes time, and even when it looks like it is healed on the surface, it is what is underneath that really needs to heal. Allowing yourself the ability to grieve over relationships, experiences, and wrongdoings is just one element of the healing process.

The first step is recognizing that there is something that needs to be healed in the first place. Identification is the first part of this process. The second is being willing.

Families, no matter how big or small, all have broken pieces that need mending. Whether the act(s) was intentional or unrealized, the pain is there. These pages were written because of memories and stories that did not always feel good to admit out loud, but that did not mean they did not exist. I held on to these memories for years out of fear of what they might do if they were released into the atmosphere and the shame of admitting that this was a broken piece of my story.

What I have learned throughout this healing process is that it is my story for a reason, and it is up to me to decide what to do with it. My story is like that of so many others, some of whom are still unable to heal. Healing brings freedom. Now, in my mid thirties, I can speak freely knowing that it is in fact, my truth. I think that we have tricked ourselves into believing that if we do not say things out loud, that somehow they do not exist.

I challenge you, if you are reading this, to commit to yourself to take the steps toward healing. Make the decision today. Do not worry about how long it will take or the outcome, but rather get started. Whether you have someone to talk it through with or not, do this for you. It took me years to want to begin this process, knowing that I had some inner work to do, but here I am. I understand that it starts with me. If you have a journal, this is a good place for you to reflect on healing and what that might look like for you.

Generational habits, whether good or bad, have to begin with someone and continue with someone. You have the ability to make the choice for that someone to be you. It is going to be hard work, but it is possible. If you believe in therapy, make the call today and schedule your first appointment. If you prefer group sessions, research and find a group related to your issue/challenge. Whatever it is, you can make the choice today to get it done. Be encouraged.

I wish healing were easy. Healing can be a long and painful process. I had to do some healing in order to be able to write this book. I had to do some forgiving as well. What I can tell you is that when you take control over your tomorrow and you choose instead of letting things just be, you experience a totally different level of power. If no one else tells you, I believe in you. You could have stopped reading a long time ago, but since you are here, that tells me that you desire to heal. Perhaps you just might not know how. Begin to write your thoughts out, just like I did. It does not have to be perfect. It just has to be pure and from the heart.

Fathers: It is not too late to heal from your own trauma. If you can take the first step to call or visit your child, go for it. Regardless of what was done in the past, tomorrow is a new, fresh start. Break the cycle that might be ongoing in your family and choose to be vulnerable. Choose to say you apologize for any wrongdoing. No expectations, just vulnerability.

Daughters: Be open to forgiveness. Be willing to listen. Some of what you are experiencing might be a reflection of your father's own childhood trauma. While nothing is perfect, it cannot be undone. You can choose what forgiveness looks like from here on out. I encourage you to try as I have done. No expectations, just willingness.

Legacy

THROUGHOUT MY ENTIRE LIFE, MY FATHER ALWAYS STRESSED
the importance of leaving a legacy. He would actually sit our family
down, with quotes adorning our basement wall, telling us about this
legacy he was building. None of us believed what he was saying. It
never mattered to him whether we believed him or not. He kept talking
about the legacy of the Scott family. I will admit that at times I looked
at him in judgment because of what I saw on the outside, and I would
say to myself, how is it that you are building a legacy when you are not
around for the children you have today. What I know and understand
now is that he believed it enough to share it with us, and he knew that
if he said it enough, we would catch on and take the baton and run with
it. The legacy he talked about was one where we embraced our culture
and who we were, stuck together as a family, and created generational
wealth for those to come. I never wanted to be an entrepreneur fully,
but I always had his spirit of entrepreneurship inside of me.

As a child, I was always on the go and labeled as the kid who
talked too much. What I did not know was that some years later, people
would pay me to speak. The legacy started to become clearer. This was
the legacy that my father spoke of. He always strived for greatness and
hoped that we would all catch on. Some may say it took him passing

away for us to want to continue his legacy, but I disagree. The start of me writing this book came months before my father had died. I was frustrated because I could not finish the book. I kept starting, writing a page or two, and then deleting it all and putting it down. I did not know why that kept happening, and as a writer that is the most frustrating aspect about writing. You just want to write and release your project to the world.

What I know now about the legacy my father wanted to leave was for people to know his story and some of what plagued him and so many other families in our communities. He wanted more than anything for his name to live on and for all of the work that he did to not have been in vain. Legacy (n) by definition means the following: *a gift by will, especially of money or other personal property* (Merriam-Webster Collegiate Dictionary, 2003). When my sisters and I went to retrieve my father's belongings after he had passed, there were four keys and four pennies in his pocket. We took one of each. We knew that this was all he had to his name when he died. While that might sound sad and unfortunate, what I want you to know is that he left much more than that. He left purpose, drive, knowledge, and his life's testimony, which was priceless. It is now up to us to continue to go on and continue what my father started. And so, his life was not in vain, and there will be a legacy for generations to come.

The Answer

Funny how God works. After my father passed away, I was fortunate to go through some of his items he had tucked away in a storage unit, and I came across his memoir. It was no easy feat, finding this book of raw and edited notes from various stages in his life. I sat with it in my hands, not knowing what its contents entailed. Little did I know, the answers to most of my questions were already written down for me. What is even funnier is I have memories of my father being up late at night when I was very young, and I recall asking him what he was writing. He replied, "It's Daddy's memoir, *As the Pendulum Swings*." Now, out of all the things my father said to me growing up, why did this one sentence stick out to me so much? Why is that memory so vivid? I can even smell the cigarette smoke and see his eyes red from being up all night when he said it.

What I did not know and what he did not know was that while this was the beginning of me thinking about all of the questions I had, he was literally sitting at his computer answering them. You see, this book was part of his destiny and had no choice but to find me. After so many years of being frustrated with not knowing who my father was or why he was the way that he was, the answers finally found me. Little did he know, he was answering all of my questions so that I would not be stuck in unforgiveness, and I could continue on with the legacy he wanted so deeply to build. Holding that book that was unfinished in my hand felt like a gift. I would forever have the story that my father wanted to tell. I am certain that parts of his life he was ashamed to tell. Moreover, as he wrote, he had to relive the pain of his childhood. He was allowing his life and thoughts to be on display, just as I am doing right now and allowing space for readers to critique my work. As a writer, this is what it takes. You have to be willing to be vulnerable and fearless.

Once you have released your work, it is a shared piece open to interpretation. I bet my father did not know that is what he was doing when he started writing his book over thirty years ago. Who would have ever thought I would take his work and run with it, only after I was able to first understand him more.

Selections from Daddy's Memoir: *As The Pendulum Swings* {unpublished}

What I Can Remember from My Childhood

"Starting from childhood, where we are thrust into our environment, we somehow find ourselves as we pass through both triumph and despair. Ultimately we recognize our calling and are propelled into a dynamic destiny."

—Howard John Scott

I CAN SAY I WAS BORN TO NEITHER TRIUMPH NOR DESPAIR. I viewed my family situation as fairly normal—however *normal* is defined. We lived in a two-family house in the west end of New Rochelle, New York, occupying the second and third floors, as well as the basement. Not normal, however, was the age of my parents when I was born. My mother, Helen Charlotte Long Scott, was thirty-nine, and my father, Jesse James Scott, was approaching his sixties.

Medical technology had not advanced to the point that a doctor could tell a pregnant woman what she was carrying. I can only imagine her surprise—and shock—at delivering twins that April 1958 when my twin brother and I were born. My father had another family in

New Jersey and was in our lives on a part-time basis. Although he was present on special occasions, my mother, for the most part, was left to care for their four sons on her own.

From early on, John and I learned quickly how easy it was to do whatever we wanted, whenever we wanted. Like many Black families in America, we had an absentee father and a single mother head of household who raised us. To make ends meet, our mother worked as a housekeeper for two well-to-do White families who lived in the north end of New Rochelle. We were also dependent on the welfare system for survival. Although the system was intended to help the disadvantaged, many believed the monthly handouts were designed to keep those who lived in urban communities pitiable. The monthly welfare check made certain the rent was paid, but barely anything else.

The chapter title reflects the bifurcated nature of my early childhood years, between the time I was five and eleven years old. I often refer to my early childhood as a string of episodes of delinquency—one after another. I should start, however, by saying I discovered my entrepreneurial spirit first, at the tender age of five, when John and I paid an occasional visit to the local beer garden and danced for quarters. That was not our first introduction to money, but until then, we had never really grasped the value of it. . . . These experiences turned something on within me—an appreciation of the almighty dollar and the drive to get my hands on as much as I could for myself, without regard for the legality or the consequences.

It was not until a couple of years had passed that I put my industrious talent to work and learned to take advantage of opportunities that presented themselves along the way.

Woodfield Cottage was the state's answer for juvenile delinquents, designed to house kids aged ten to sixteen who were awaiting action from the court. The center focuses on rehabilitation, regular education, skills training, and therapy services. But all this activity occurs behind very tall, very thick walls. They boast arts and sports programs, as well as mentorship talks from former residents and semi-high-profile visitors. Woodfield was featured in a 1997 *New York Times* article on the topic of not giving up on youth offenders.

We knew Woodfield. We had heard of kids caught at the wrong time and sent there. If you do enough of anything, you will get what is coming to you—good or bad—the reward will come. John and I learned that fast.

We got fifteen minutes with our mother. We were as tall as her at that time and our pampering days were over. We sat on those gray metal chairs as she assured us we would be okay, that it would not be for long. The only response we had to that was silence. A knock on the door broke it. *Time's up.* And suddenly, I was marching to my death. All my past wrongs came sauntering into my head to the beat of my steps.

Quiet time at Woodfield usually meant intermingling with our peers. But, more often than not, I found myself at the lonesome bookcase in the corner. I thumbed through history-filled pages of the *Negro Almanac.* And every day, at three o'clock I huddled, spellbound, over page after page of Black history. I may not have recognized it as such at the time, but those books held a vice grip over me, as I sat for hours curled up with the world in my lap. *Harry Potter* was one thing, but reading through history, understanding that the story is true, and that it all leads up to where you sit now, intoxicated me in my innocence. My first foray was into the faces I recognized: Harriet Tubman, Malcolm

X, and Martin Luther King Jr. Their bios quickly became go-to knowledge for me as I moved on to the names and faces I did not recognize: David Walker, Nat Turner, Marcus Garvey, and others. I devoured the knowledge of such facts that a Black man had been minted on a US coin in the 1940s.

In time, something occurred to me that shook my world. The rough behavior that had resulted in me sitting in this detention center far from home was not by accident. I was in that corner with those books for a reason. I felt a profound and visceral sense of purpose, of somehow being chosen. Fate had designed that I would go to Woodfield Cottage. And there I would learn about the heritage no one had ever shown me before. A love of reading and my own desire to write was born out of my discovery of those history books. My calling was brightly written on those pages of "blackness." Some thirty years later, when I found myself a publisher, those circumstances were a far cry from the rough-edged rock I was when I first arrived at Woodfield Cottage. Painful and frightening as it had been, that experience provided me with something I would not have received any other way: a chance to change.

And suddenly, that callous rock would find himself a jewel.

Howard's Firsts

AT AGE SIXTEEN, I SET UP MY FIRST PLASTICS BUSINESS, Fantastic Plastics, at the leased location in Orange, New Jersey. My brother John and I moved out of our mother's house and into the third-floor room of my father's apartment. Mike [my friend from the neighborhood] stayed behind in Mount Vernon with my mother, as he was still working at the plating company where he and I had first met. In a year's time, however, Mike would join John and me in New Jersey.

I had not yet quit my job at AIN Plastics, and for a time, I was putting in eighteen-hour workdays, driving back and forth between my full-time plastics job in New York and my start-up company in New Jersey. I hated to quit the security and reliability of a weekly paycheck. This went on for four months. The drive between Orange and Mount Vernon took about seventy-five minutes, and cost me a lot in gas and tolls, not to mention my own physical well-being.

One day, my brother finally said to me, "Howard, the business needs you here." All along, my reluctance to quit was due solely to the fact that I was completely on my own. But then two things happened that aided in my decision to leave the comfort of AIN: (1) Public Law 95-507 had, in 1978, been amended to encourage large contracting agencies and businesses to place subcontracts with small businesses and minority firms, which we were, and (2) my twin had gone into the New York City and secured two big jobs—one for ten thousand dollars and another worth five thousand dollars. Things started to look up.

Shortly thereafter, the local newspaper ran an article on the business. We were riding high with all the business and attention.

One day, I heard three little words that would very quickly affect how I conducted business going forward. The words were: *Success Motivation Institute*. This program by Paul J. Meyer of Waco, Texas, told me to put down my boom box, pick up their cardboard box, and find inside the keys to success. More specifically, they offered a program called the Dynamics of Personal Goal Setting. The program promised to help me set my goals, develop a plan for achieving them, build a conscious desire to reach my goals, gain confidence in myself and my abilities, and follow through with unwavering commitment. At just eighteen years of age and visions of success looming ahead, I purchased the program and followed it step by step.

They were right. Not only did I buy the program, I bought *into* it. I stored their teachings in my head and before long had ingrained the concepts that, as long as I adhered to them, guaranteed me success. I was a good student. I listened to the course tapes, read through all the materials, and set my goals. Over the years, I would revisit this program multiple times, mostly after finding myself down (and out) and realizing I needed help to pick myself up again.

The very first goal I planned to achieve was to obtain a four-door, baby blue Mercedes Benz, just like the one my former boss at AIN Plastics had. I loved that car. Part two of that goal was to achieve it by age thirty. Was that goal too lofty? Apparently not. You see, I put into practice the Success Motivation Institute program steps, and my business grew by leaps and bounds. Contracts came in from IBM, DuPont, General Motors, Conrail, and dozens more. The business got so busy we hired at least eighteen workers. Yes, by the age of eighteen, I had eighteen people working for me. Success came fast and it came furious. In just four short years, we had grown to be a million-dollar business. I rode the wave of success all the way, and by the age of twenty-two, I was at the top. I had made my first million and was riding the high for all it was worth . . . and more.

By the time I turned twenty-five, I had lost it all. I was flat broke. Everything I had worked so hard to achieve for over ten years had been ruined because of my drinking and drug habits. Devastated was the only word to describe how I felt at the string of what I call my firsts: my first love—plastics, my first success—build a business from the ground up by age twenty-two, my first million as an entrepreneur, and . . . my first fall. Amazingly, I was able to buy a house through a city auction. Even though it had no heat or running water, I owned it free and clear. The house, though, became both a blessing and a curse—a blessing because it provided a roof over my head, a curse because I kept myself locked away inside for six months. I drank continuously, sleeping by day, feeding my habit by night. My situation had become so bad, I even stopped bathing and moved around the house like a zombie.

Homeless in Atlanta

IT WAS THE FIRST I HAD EVER SEEN IN ATLANTA, GEORGIA. I HAD arrived seven days earlier via Greyhound Bus Lines. Atlanta was not what I expected, and certainly not all that it was cracked up to be, with one exception—the weather. That Sunday afternoon in the fall of 2003, the sky was clear and the gentle breeze felt comfortable in the sun. The journey from South Carolina to Atlanta took nine hours and thirty minutes and included an unusual number of stops along the way. I sat at a window seat behind an older gentleman who hummed spirituals from the time he boarded in Fayetteville until the minute we arrived in Atlanta. I suppose you could say he was a spiritual man, but I can't say I was in the same frame of mind as he was. In any case, I listened to him feed his spiritual appetite the entire trip.

Five minutes prior to our arrival in Atlanta, the driver announced we would soon be pulling into the bus terminal. At that, the hummer sang a familiar hymn, "Back Home." As we stood to disembark, he turned to me and smiled. "It sure feels good to be back home," he said. I smiled back and told him I agreed with the sentiment. I guessed his humming wasn't so bad after all.

Buses pulled in and out of the busy terminal. The passengers on my bus were cheerful at having finally arrived, and we stood in anticipation as the bus driver opened the hatch where our suitcases had been stored. My singer friend stood beside me. He pointed and said, "Sonny, would you get that dark green suitcase there for me?" I pulled his suitcase out along with those of several other passengers. I picked up my own black duffle and walked into the terminal building.

My first impression, beyond the noise and bustle inside, was that the floor could use a broom and a mop. I perused the smallish bus depot and estimated that about forty of the approximately one hundred plastic seats in the waiting area were occupied by men who appeared to be asleep, many slumped in their seats with their heads resting on their shoulder. They certainly did not appear to be waiting for a bus. I concluded that these men must be homeless. I noticed a bag on the floor beside each man, stuffed to the top with clothing. If I did not know better, I would think the place was a homeless shelter rather than the Atlanta bus terminal.

I turned and walked back out, scared with the sudden realization that I, too, was homeless, a fact that had not occurred to me when I boarded the bus in South Carolina. Over the years, I had traveled a fair amount, but never with a meager fifteen dollars in my pocket or with no intended destination or no one to call upon my arrival. Only homeless people travel like that. And now, I was one of them. I had joined the ranks of the homeless, hundreds of miles away from family and friends.

A force had beckoned me to Atlanta—something or someone had prodded me to make this trip, and so I did. Perhaps I could have traveled to another city, but everything inside me told me the time had come to begin a renewed life, and Atlanta, Georgia, would be the first stop.

Although I was homeless, I felt comforted. I felt an inner peace and acceptance, as the Spirit of God directed me along. In my serenity, I was certain I was finally going to change my life from the bottom up. Though the pendulum had been swinging away from me, I had faith I was finally on the right path—I knew God was with me.

Victory House

I WAS SITTING IN THE SHADE OF A PECAN TREE AS THE SUN SET, waiting to get into the Jefferson Street Shelter. As usual, I had been reading, feeding my mind with an extra dose of spiritual mental fine tuning. Nearby, I heard two young men talking with another man who, like me, was waiting to get into the shelter. The men were clean shaven and well dressed, wearing neckties and sports jackets, so they were clearly not seeking to sleep at Jefferson. I sensed from their enthusiastic tone they were offering the man an opportunity. At their pronouncement of the name of Jesus, I got up and went to where these men were talking.

The two young men had rolled up in a fifteen-passenger van and were inviting those of us they suspected were homeless to join them for a meal and a place to sleep, and also to attend church services. I heard them mention Victory House, but I didn't care. I was the first to say yes. Another six after me also accepted the offer. I grabbed my duffle bag and walked up the hill to where the van sat idling. As we pulled away, I wondered why more of the men waiting in the Jefferson Street Shelter parking lot did not take this opportunity. Was it because they didn't want to attend church?

We drove to another shelter and parked. The two recruiters jumped out and launched into their spiel. In under five minutes another seven men had climbed into the van. Now full, we were ready to make the drive across town to Victory House. In the parking area around the back of the building, we all got out of the van and marched into the house through a makeshift kitchen and dining area. I was still beaming with enthusiasm and looking forward to learning more about Victory House.

One large dining table accommodated up to twelve people, and other tables around the room held up to another twelve. We all sat at the large table, as instructed. Before long, the two young men who had recruited us brought in our plates of food. This organization clearly lacked the personnel, finances, and resources of other similar shelters, as these two men appeared to be doing just about everything. Dinner was spaghetti, two slices of bread, and a small cup of juice. Thankfully, I was served first, as I wanted to clean up before the church service. After being outside and walking around in the hot sun all day, I was sweaty and in much need of a shower, as were all the other men I rode with in the van. I wasted no time devouring my helping of spaghetti and finishing well ahead of the others.

I was taken to the second floor where the bathroom was located. The room was pint-sized and in bad need of renovation, but the water felt good on my skin and refreshed me nicely. After drying off, I realized I had left my duffle bag downstairs in the dining room. Rather than put my soiled clothes back on, I wrapped my towel around my waist to go and retrieve my bag. I picked up my dirty clothes to drop them in the room where they had indicated I would be sleeping and noticed my duffle bag was on the bed. My first thought was that one of those multitasking recruiters had pitched in again, only this time as a butler.

Inside the bag, I found a suitable pair of black pants and a white shirt that needed to be pressed. Rather than worry about ironing it, I put on a vest that covered most of the wrinkles. One look in the mirror let me know I was appropriately dressed for church service. I smiled with approval.

Back downstairs, I joined the others in the living room who were watching television. Thirty minutes later, our two recruiters appeared and spoke to us about what to expect at the church service.

"We dance. We shout. We do the holy walk."

Oh, my God, I thought. Better put your seatbelts on.

"The service starts at eight, but we get there an hour early to pray."

The more details they shared about their church, the less interested I became, until my enthusiasm was completely gone. I soon figured out that this was not just any old church, and that we would be there a while. I was right. The service did not end until half past ten.

That was three and a half hours of church. I had, in fact, overdosed on Victory House.

Nothing Changes If
Nothing Changes

CHANGE IS INEVITABLE. NOTHING STAYS THE SAME. THE BOOK of Ecclesiastes tells us there is a time for everything, that change will happen whether we like it or not. So much is said in the second verse of the third chapter of Ecclesiastes: "A time to be born and a time to die."

Consider the first part of the phrase: a time to be born. What does that say? What is born? The dictionary defines the word *born* as that which exists as a result of birth. So, what is birth? Birth refers to a beginning, origin, creation, or extraction. If that is true, change must be birthed. If we give birth to change, then and only then can we change that which we have birthed.

I lost—and missed—a lot through my years of abuse of alcohol and drugs. I recall the night my mother died. I was using, and received a phone call from my cousin who broke the news. So lost was I in my own plight, I had not even taken the time to see or talk to my mother in eight or nine months before she died. It would be days before I felt the true impact of her death. I lost my two oldest brothers to the same disease that afflicts me. In their case, one was a heroin user (they found needles on him at the time of his death) and the other died from AIDS.

I recall the recommendation of my counselor all those years ago. "Believe in a power greater than yourself." Everyone is different, and each person's *higher power* may be unique, but I can honestly say I am a believer. I would never have been able to see or understand how I could possibly have escaped the death trap into which I had fallen without the vigilance of someone or something that saved me from myself.

{Selections from} Written Work, Publications, and Speaking Engagements

- 1990–1998 – Publisher/Editor *Visions Weekly*
- September 1995 – Start of *Visions Monthly* newsmagazine to capture "positive news for a change."
- February 1997 – Start of *Visions Weekly*, but did not survive due to lack of paid advertising, closed July 1997.
- 1998–2000 – Editor of Good News CT Press
- 2001–2003 – Principal at Legacy Media

Millennium Magazine

LATE 2000 *VISIONS MONTHLY NEWSMAGAZINE* CHANGED TO *Twin Visions* weekly, with Howard as publisher. Circulated to all five wards in Newark and covers news in urban cities throughout Northern New Jersey. The news was intended to inspire, educate, inform, and stay with the reader. We had fifty thousand weekly readers, male/female, black/white, age eighteen to seventy.

Howard publishes/contributes to *Twin Visions Weekly* (2000–2001):

- 1/21/2000–1/27/2000 – The Black Press

- 6/16/2000–6/22/2000 – Black Postage, A Rare Find

- 8/11/2000–8/17/2000 – The Black Press – Friendship or Foeship

- 8/25/2000–8/31/2000 – Can We Count on You?

- 10/20/2000–10/26/2000 – Our Growth Depends on Your Support

- 10/27/2000–11/2/2000 – Our Growth Depends on Your Support

- 11/3/2000–11/9/2000 – Forty-cents and a Dream

- 1/5/2001–1/11/2001 – Continuing Our Ancestor's Legacy

- 1/12/2001–1/18/2001 – Continuing Our Ancestor's Legacy

- 6/22/2001–6/28/2001 – From the Very Beginning: How the Black Press Was Born

Legacy Media Group (2005-2007)

Visions Metro Weekly, a Legacy Media Group Publication, Howard Scott, Editor in Chief

- 12/16/2005–12/22/2005 – The Miracle and Tradition Behind Chanukah

- 2/17/2006–2/23/2006 – America Says Diversity Works But in Reality, It Is Still a Work in Progress

- 3/3/2006–3/9/2006 – Why Black History Means So Much

- 1/12/2007–1/18/2007 – Our Story

Miscellaneous Work

- Lee County Observer (5/12/2004) – Article "Visiting Inmates, He Totes 'Guns' for God"; receives email request from Sandra Gamble (6/7/2004) to speak at Horizon Addiction Treatment Unit Program on 6/24 at Lee Correctional Facility, which he accepts —The program serves to transition adult male offenders back into society.

- Speaker at Family Reunion (8/5/2006) – West family looked for someone who was "dynamic and rich in the black culture" to speak at the affair—A positive message on black culture and the black family.

- Twin Visions Publications youth program: Motivating Our Youth to Excel—to teach youth to excel in school and in their personal life. Children will learn the ingredients of success through personal goal-setting that will transfer each goal to appropriate areas of their life. Children will learn their history and about those before them: Malcolm X, Martin Luther King, Sojourner Truth, Harriet Tubman, Mary McCloud Bethume, and so on. Teach a child a nation is our goal so we must invest in our children, regain their respect, and let them know we care.

- What Makes a Successful Entrepreneur? "Everything I've Ever Wanted" (May 2006), a First Friday Networking & Advancement session.

The Final Letter {To My Father}

DADDY,

I wish I could tell you there was a different ending to your story. I wish I could say yours ended in triumph. What I can say is, you are now at rest. Unbeknownst to you, I am reading your memoir and all of the questions I had as a child and young adult you answered for me here. After reading about your childhood, I got a glimpse of your family, misfortunes, and grief you experienced even as a young boy. I now, too, understand the longing you had for your father that you never received. I understand your hustle and grind now that I know you didn't have education. Your brilliance still amazes me. You achieved so much and struggled with your own addictions. You hid it so well. I can only imagine the real pain you felt at night. You tried, Daddy. You tried, and for that I thank you. You were a believer, and your legacy truly lives on. Thank you for the tools you gave me to be the resilient woman I am today. Rest well Daddy. Your Baby Girl.

DEAR GOD,

Grant me the serenity to accept the things I can not change, the courage to change the things I can, and the wisdom to know the difference . . .